A CATECHISM OF CHRISTIAN DOCTRINE

*All booklets are published thanks to the
generous support of the members of the
Catholic Truth Society*

CATHOLIC TRUTH SOCIETY
PUBLISHERS TO THE HOLY SEE

CONTENTS

Imprimatur
John Cardinal Heenan, Archbishop of Westminster, 18 July 1971.

Acknowledgements
Approved by the Archbishops and Bishops of England and Wales, and directed to be used in all their dioceses. First published, 1889. Revised, 1985. Millennium edition, 1997. This Jubilee edition, 1999.
This edition of the 'Penny Catechism' should not be considered as an abridged version of the Catechism of the Catholic Church (1994).

Summary of the Catechism of
❧ Catholic Doctrine ❧

I. Faith

Regarding Man:
- His first beginning (1-5)
- His last end (6-8) (128-134)

The Belief:
- In God the Father (9-30)
- In Jesus Christ (31-76)
- In the Holy Spirit (77-82)
- In the Holy Catholic Church (83-109)

II. Hope

The Our Father: The Seven Blessings
- to be hoped for (135-140)
- to be prayed for (141-157)

The Hail Mary: Assistance of the Blessed Virgin and of the Angels and Saints (158-168)

III. Charity

The Commandments:
- of God (169-227)
- of the Church (228-248)

IV. The Sacraments

The Seven Great Means of Grace

Corresponding to:
- the birth (265-261)
- the growth (262-265)
- the nourishment (266-280)
- the medicine (110-127) (281-300)
- the journey of the soul (301-304)
- the Christian Priesthood (305)
- the Christian Family (306-312)

V. Christian Life

- The Virtues and contrary Vices (313-332)
- The Christian's Rule of Life (333-354)
- The Christian's Daily Exercise (355-370)

The Spiritual House of the Soul is built up in time and solemnly dedicated in eternity.

Faith is the foundation.

Hope the walls.

Charity the roof, or covering.

The Sacraments are the great means of grace, or the chief instruments required for the building.

The Virtues, the Christian's Rule of Life, and the Daily Exercise, may be likened to the adornment and furniture of the House.

(St. Augustine, 20 Sermon in verb. sap.).

– ❧ Let us go Forward in Hope! ❧ –

His Holiness, Pope John Paul II

A new millennium is opening before the Church like a vast ocean upon which we shall venture, relying on the help of Christ. The Son of God, who became incarnate two thousand years ago out of love for humanity, is at work even today: we need discerning eyes to see this and, above all, a generous heart to become the instruments of his work... Now, the Christ whom we have contemplated and loved bids us to set out once more on our journey: "Go therefore and make disciples out of all nations, baptising in the name of the Father, and of the Son and of the Holy Spirit"
(Mt 28:19) (John Paul II, Novo Millennio Ineunte)

Why do you seek me Lord?

In the Incarnation God himself speaks to me. By becoming one of us in history, Christ fully reveals man to man himself and makes his supreme calling clear by revealing the mystery of the Father's love. It is here Christianity differs from all other religions through which man has long searched for his God. It is God who comes in person to speak to me of himself and show me the path by which He may be reached.

Christ incarnate is the fulfilment of the yearning present in all the religions of all mankind! It is the mystery of grace. In Christ religion is no longer a blind search for God, but the response of faith to God who reveals himself to me. I can speak to God as my Creator and Father. So God not only speaks to me but seeks me out! The Incarnation attests that God has gone in search of me, because he loves me eternally and wishes to raise me in Christ to the dignity of an adoptive son. Why do you search for me as a special possession unlike any other creature!

I turned away from you, I allowed myself to be led astray by the enemy, Satan, who persuaded me that I too was God, capable of knowing good and evil, making the world according to my own will without reference to the divine will. How you have searched for me! Wanting me to abandon the path of evil that I have taken, to overcome the evil which is found in human history. Overcoming evil: this is the meaning of the Redemption. My Redemption!

(Adapted from *Tertio Millennio Adveniente* John Paul II)

❧ FAITH ❧

Faith in God

1. Who made you?

God made me.

2. Why did God make you?

God made me to know him, love him and serve him in this world, and to be happy with him for ever in the next.

3. To whose image and likeness did God make you?

God made me to his own image and likeness.

4. Is this likeness to God in your body, or in your soul?

This likeness to God is chiefly in my soul.

5. How is your soul like to God?

My soul is like to God because it is a spirit, and is immortal.

6. What do you mean when you say that your soul is immortal?

When I say my soul is immortal, I mean that my soul can never die.

7. Of which must you take more care, of your body or of your soul?

I must take more care of my soul; for Christ has said, 'What does it profit a man if he gains the whole world, and suffers the loss of his own soul?' *(Matt. 16:26)*

8. What must you do to save your soul?

To save my soul I must worship God by Faith, Hope and Charity; that is, I must believe in him, I must hope in him, and I must love him with my whole heart.

9. What is faith?

Faith is a supernatural gift of God, which enables us to believe without doubting whatever God has revealed.

10. Why must you believe whatever God has revealed?

I must believe whatever God has revealed because God is the very truth, and can neither deceive nor be deceived.

11. How are you to know what God has revealed?

I am to know what God has revealed by the testimony, teaching, and authority of the Catholic Church.

12. Who gave the Catholic Church divine authority to teach?

Jesus Christ gave the Catholic Church divine authority to teach, when he said, 'Go therefore, make disciples of all the nations'. *(Matt. 28:19)*

The Apostles' Creed

13. What are the chief things which God has revealed?

The chief things which God has revealed are contained in the Apostles' Creed.

14. Say the Apostles' Creed

I believe in God, the Father Almighty, Creator of heaven and earth; - and in Jesus Christ, his only Son, our Lord; - who was conceived by the Holy Spirit, born of the Virgin Mary; - suffered under Pontius Pilate, was crucified, dead, and buried; - he descended into hell; the third day he rose again from the dead; - he ascended into heaven; is seated at the right hand of God the Father Almighty; - from thence he shall come to judge the living and the dead. - I believe in the Holy Spirit; - the Holy Catholic Church; the Communion of Saints; - the forgiveness of sins; - the resurrection of the body; - and life everlasting. Amen.

15. How is the Apostles' Creed divided?

The Apostles' Creed is divided into twelve parts or articles.

First Article of the Creed

16. What is the first article of the Creed?

The first article of the Creed is, 'I believe in God, the Father Almighty, Creator of heaven and earth'.

17. What is God?

God is the supreme Spirit, who alone exists of himself, and is infinite in all perfection.

18. Why is God called Almighty?

God is called 'Almighty' because he can do all things; 'For God everything is possible'. *(Matt. 19:26)*

19. Why is God called Creator of heaven and earth?

God is called 'Creator of heaven and earth' because he made heaven and earth, and all things, out of nothing, by his word.

20. Had God any beginning?

God had no beginning: he always was, he is, and he always will be.

21. Where is God?

God is everywhere.

22. Does God know and see all things?

God knows and sees all things, even our most secret thoughts.

23. Had God any body?

God has no body; he is a spirit.

24. Is there only one God?

There is only one God.

25. Are there three Persons in God?

There are three Persons in God: God the Father, God the Son, and God the Holy Spirit.

26. Are these three Persons three Gods?

These three Persons are not three Gods: the Father, the Son, and the Holy Spirit are all one and the same God.

27. What is the mystery of the Three Persons in one God called?

The mystery of the three Persons in one God is called the mystery of the Blessed Trinity.

28. What do you mean by a mystery?

By a mystery I mean a truth which is above reason, but revealed by God.

29. Is there any likeness to the Blessed Trinity in your soul?

There is this likeness to the Blessed Trinity in my soul: that as in one God there are three Persons, so in my one soul there are three powers.

30. Which are the three powers of your soul?

The three powers of my soul are my memory, my understanding, and my will.

The Second Article of the Creed

31. What is the second article of the Creed?

The second article of the Creed is, 'and in Jesus Christ, his only Son, our Lord'.

32. Who is Jesus Christ?

Jesus Christ is God the Son, made man for us.

33. Is Jesus Christ truly God?

Jesus Christ is truly God.

34. Why is Jesus Christ truly God?

Jesus Christ is truly God because he has one and the same nature with God the Father.

35. Was Jesus Christ always God?

Jesus Christ was always God, born of the Father from all eternity.

36. Which Person of the Blessed Trinity is Jesus Christ?

Jesus Christ is the Second Person of the Blessed Trinity.

37. Is Jesus Christ truly man?

Jesus Christ is truly man.

38. Why is Jesus Christ truly man?

Jesus Christ is truly man because he has the nature of man, having a body and soul like ours.

39. Was Jesus Christ always man?

Jesus Christ was not always man. He has been man only from the time of his Incarnation.

40. What do you mean by the Incarnation?

I mean by the Incarnation that God the Son took to himself the nature of man: 'the Word was made Flesh'. *(John 1:14)*

41. How many natures are there in Jesus Christ?

There are two natures in Jesus Christ, the nature of God and the nature of man.

42. Is there only one Person in Jesus Christ?

There is only one Person in Jesus Christ, which is the Person of God the Son.

43. Why was God the Son made man?

God the Son was made man to redeem us from sin and hell, and to teach us the way to heaven.

44. What does the holy name Jesus mean?

The holy name Jesus means Saviour. *(Matt. 1:21)*

45. What does the name Christ mean?

The name Christ means Anointed.

46. Where is Jesus Christ?

As God, Jesus Christ is everywhere. As God made man, he is in heaven, and in the Blessed Sacrament of the Altar.

The Third Article of the Creed

47. What is the third article of the Creed?

The third article of the Creed is, 'who was conceived by the Holy Spirit, born of the Virgin Mary'.

48. What does the third article mean?

The third article means that God the Son took a Body and Soul like ours, in the womb of the Blessed Virgin Mary, by the power of the Holy Spirit.

49. Had Jesus Christ any father on earth?

Jesus Christ had no father on earth: St Joseph was only his guardian or foster-father.

50. Where was our Saviour born?

Our Saviour was born in a stable at Bethlehem.

51. On what day was our Saviour born?

Our Saviour was born on Christmas Day.

The Fourth Article of the Creed

52. What is the fourth article of the Creed?

The fourth article of the Creed is, 'suffered under Pontius Pilate, was crucified, dead, and buried'.

53. What were the chief sufferings of Christ?

The chief sufferings of Christ were: first, his agony, and his sweat of blood in the Garden; secondly, his being scourged at the pillar, and crowned with thorns; and thirdly his carrying his cross, his crucifixion, and his death between two thieves.

54. What are the chief sufferings of our Lord called?

The chief sufferings of our Lord are called the Passion of Jesus Christ.

55. Why did our Saviour suffer?

Our Saviour suffered to atone for our sins, and to purchase for us eternal life.

56. Why is Jesus Christ called our Redeemer?

Jesus Christ is called our Redeemer because his precious blood is the price by which we were ransomed.

57. On what day did our Saviour die?

Our Saviour died on Good Friday.

58. Where did our Saviour die?

Our Saviour died on Mount Calvary.

59. Why do we make the sign of the cross?

We make the sign of the cross - first, to put us in mind of the Blessed Trinity; and secondly to remind us that God the Son died for us on the Cross.

60. In making the sign of the cross how are we reminded of the Blessed Trinity?

In making the sign of the cross we are reminded of the Blessed Trinity by the words, 'In the name of the Father, and of the Son, and of the Holy Spirit'.

61. In making the sign of the cross how are we reminded that Christ died for us on the Cross?

In making the sign of the cross we are reminded that Christ died for us on the Cross by the very form of the cross which we make upon ourselves.

The Fifth Article of the Creed

62. What is the fifth article of the Creed?

The fifth article of the Creed is, 'he descended into hell; the third day he rose again from the dead'.

63. What do you mean by the words, 'he descended into hell'?

By the words 'he descended into hell' I mean that, as soon as Christ was dead, his blessed Soul went down into that part of hell called Limbo.

64. What do you mean by Limbo?

By Limbo I mean a place of rest, where the souls of the just who died before Christ were detained.

65. Why were the souls of the just detained in Limbo?

The souls of the just were detained in Limbo because they could not go up to the kingdom of heaven till Christ had opened it for them.

66. What do you mean by the words, 'the third day he rose again from the dead'?

By the words, 'the third day he rose again from the dead', I mean that, after Christ had been dead and buried part of three days, he raised his blessed Body to life again on the third day.

67. On what day did Christ rise again from the dead?

Christ rose again from the dead on Easter Sunday.

The Sixth Article of the Creed

68. What is the sixth article of the Creed?

The sixth article of the Creed is, 'he ascended into heaven; is seated at the right hand of God the Father Almighty'.

69. What do you mean by the words, 'he ascended into heaven'?

By the words, 'he ascended into heaven', I mean that our Saviour went up Body and Soul into heaven on Ascension Day, forty days after his resurrection.

70. What do you mean by the words, 'is seated at the right hand of God the Father Almighty'?

By the words, 'is seated at the right hand of God the Father Almighty', I do not mean that God the Father has hands, for he is a spirit; but I mean that Christ, as God, is equal to the Father and, as man, is in the highest place in heaven.

The Seventh Article of the Creed

71. What is the seventh article of the Creed?

The seventh article of the Creed is, 'from thence he shall come to judge the living and the dead'.

72. When will Christ come again?

Christ will come again from heaven at the last day, to judge all mankind.

73. What are the things Christ will judge?

Christ will judge our thoughts, words, works, and omissions.

74. What will Christ say to the wicked?

Christ will say to the wicked: 'Go away from me, with your curse upon you, to the eternal fire prepared for the devil and his angels'. *(Matt. 25:41)*

75. What will Christ say to the just?

Christ will say to the just: 'Come you whom my Father has blessed, take for your heritage the kingdom prepared for you'. *(Matt. 25:34)*

76. Will every one be judged at death, as well as at the last day?

Every one will be judged at death, as well as at the last day: 'Since men only die once, and after that comes judgement'. *(Heb. 9:27)*

The Eighth Article of the Creed

77. What is the eighth article of the Creed?

The eighth article of the Creed is, 'I believe in the Holy Spirit'.

78. Who is the Holy Spirit?

The Holy Spirit is the Third Person of the Blessed Trinity.

79. From whom does the Holy Spirit proceed?

The Holy Spirit proceeds from the Father and the Son.

80. Is the Holy Spirit equal to the Father and to the Son?

The Holy Spirit is equal to the Father and to the Son, for he is the same Lord and God as they are.

81. When did the Holy Spirit come down on the Apostles?

The Holy Spirit came down on the Apostles at Pentecost, in the form that 'seemed like tongues of fire'. *(Acts 2:3)*

82. Why did the Holy Spirit come down on the Apostles?

The Holy Spirit came down on the Apostles to confirm their faith, to sanctify them, and to enable them to found the Church.

The Ninth Article of the Creed

83. What is the ninth article of the Creed?

The ninth article of the Creed is, 'the Holy Catholic Church; the Communion of Saints'.

84. What is the Catholic Church?

The Catholic Church is the union of all the faithful under one Head.

85. Who is Head of the Catholic Church?

The Head of the Catholic Church is Jesus Christ our Lord.

86. Has the Church a visible Head on earth?

The Church has a visible Head on earth - the Bishop of Rome, who is the Vicar of Christ.

87. Why is the Bishop of Rome the Head of the Church?

The Bishop of Rome is the Head of the Church because he is the successor of St Peter, whom Christ appointed to be the Head of the Church.

88. How do you know that Christ appointed St Peter to be the Head of the Church?

I know that Christ appointed St Peter to be the Head of the Church because Christ said to him: 'You are Peter, and on this rock I will build my Church. And the gates of the underworld can never hold out against it. I will give you the keys of the kingdom of heaven'. *(Matt. 16:18.19)*

89. What is the Bishop of Rome called?

The Bishop of Rome is called the Pope, which signifies Father.

90. Is the Pope the Spiritual Father of all Christians?

The Pope is the Spiritual Father of all Christians.

91. Is the Pope the Shepherd and Teacher of all Christians?

The Pope is the Shepherd and Teacher of all Christians, because Christ made St Peter the Shepherd of the whole flock when he said: 'Feed my lambs, feed my sheep'. He also prayed that his 'faith' might never fail, and commanded him to 'strengthen' his brothers. *(John 21:15-17, Luke 22:32)*

92. Is the Pope infallible?

The Pope is infallible.

93. What do you mean when you say that the Pope is infallible?

When I say that the Pope is infallible, I mean that the Pope cannot err when, as Shepherd and Teacher of all Christians, he defines a doctrine concerning faith or morals, to be held by the whole Church.

94. Has the Church of Christ any marks by which we may know her?

The Church of Christ has four marks by which we may know her: she is One - she is Holy - she is Catholic - she is Apostolic.

95. How is the Church One?

The Church is One because all her members agree in one Faith, have all the same Sacrifice and Sacraments, and are all united under one Head.

96. How is the Church Holy?

The Church is Holy because she teaches a holy doctrine, offers to all the means of holiness and is distinguished by the eminent holiness of so many thousands of her children.

97. What does the word Catholic mean?

The word Catholic means universal.

98. How is the Church Catholic or universal?

The Church is Catholic or universal because she subsists in all ages, teaches all nations, and is the one Ark of Salvation for all.

99. How is the Church Apostolic?

The Church is Apostolic because she holds the doctrines and traditions of the Apostles, and because, through the unbroken succession of her Pastors, she derives her Orders and her Mission from them.

100. Can the Church err in what she teaches?

The Church cannot err in what she teaches as to faith or morals, for she is our infallible guide in both.

101. How do you know that the Church cannot err in what she teaches?

I know that the Church cannot err in what she teaches because Christ promised that the gates of hell should never prevail against his Church; that the Holy Spirit should teach her all things; and that he himself would be with her always, even to the end of time. *(Matt. 16:18. John 14:16-26. Matt. 28:20)*

102. What do you mean by the Communion of Saints?

By the Communion of Saints I mean that all the members of the Church, in heaven, on earth, and in purgatory, are in communion with each other, as being one body in Jesus Christ.

103. How are the faithful on earth in communion with each other?

The faithful on earth are in communion with each other by professing the same faith, obeying the same authority, and assisting each other with their prayers and good works.

104. How are we in communion with the Saints in heaven?

We are in communion with the Saints in heaven by honouring them as the glorified members of the Church, and also by praying to them, and by their praying for us.

105. How are we in communion with the souls in purgatory?

We are in communion with the souls in purgatory by helping them with our prayers and good works: 'It is a holy and wholesome thought to pray for the dead, that they may be loosed from sins'. *(2 Macc. 12:46)*

106. What is purgatory?

Purgatory is a place where souls suffer for a time after death on account of their sins.

107. What souls go to purgatory?

Those souls go to purgatory that depart this life in venial sin; or that have not fully paid the debt of temporal punishment due to those sins of which the guilt has been forgiven.

108. What is temporal punishment?

Temporal punishment is punishment which will have an end, either in this world, or in the world to come.

109. How do you prove that there is a purgatory?

I prove that there is a purgatory from the constant teaching of the Church; and from the doctrine of Holy Scripture, which declares that God will render to every man according to his works; that nothing defiled shall enter heaven; and that some will be saved, 'as one who has gone through fire. *(Matt. 16:27. Apoc. 21:27. 1 Cor. 3:15)*

The Tenth Article of the Creed

110. What is the tenth article of the Creed?

The tenth article of the Creed is, 'the forgiveness of sins'.

111. What do you mean by 'the forgiveness of sins'?

By the forgiveness of sins I mean that Christ has left the power of forgiving sins to the Pastors of his Church. *(John 20:23)*

112. By what means are sins forgiven?

Sins are forgiven principally by the Sacraments of Baptism and Penance.

113. What is sin?

Sin is an offence against God, by any thought, word, deed, or omission against the law of God.

114. How many kinds of sin are there?

There are two kinds of sin, original sin and actual sin.

115. What is original sin?

Original sin is that guilt and stain of sin which we inherit from Adam, who was the origin and head of all mankind.

116. What was the sin committed by Adam?

The sin committed by Adam was the sin of disobedience when he ate the forbidden fruit.

117. Has all mankind contracted the guilt and stain of original sin?

All mankind has contracted the guilt and stain of original sin, except the Blessed Virgin and her Divine Son, through whose foreseen merits she was conceived without the least guilt or stain of original sin.

118. What is this privilege of the Blessed Virgin called?

This privilege of the Blessed Virgin is called the Immaculate Conception.

119. What is actual sin?

Actual sin is every sin which we ourselves commit.

120. How is actual sin divided?

Actual sin is divided into mortal sin and venial sin.

121. What is mortal sin?

Mortal sin is a serious offence against God.

122. Why is it called mortal sin?

It is called mortal sin because it is so serious that it kills the soul and deserves hell.

123. How does mortal sin kill the soul?

Mortal sin kills the soul by depriving it of sanctifying grace, which is the supernatural life of the soul.

124. Is it a great evil to fall into mortal sin?

It is the greatest of all evils to fall into mortal sin.

125. Where will they go who die in mortal sin?

They who die in mortal sin will go to hell for all eternity.

126. What is venial sin?

Venial sin is an offence which does not kill the soul, yet displeases God, and often leads to mortal sin.

127. Why is it called venial sin?

It is called venial sin because it is more easily pardoned than mortal sin.

The Eleventh Article of the Creed

128. What is the eleventh article of the Creed?

The eleventh article of the Creed is, 'the resurrection of the body'.

129. What do you mean by 'the resurrection of the body'?

By 'the resurrection of the body' I mean that we shall rise again with the same bodies at the day of judgment'.

The Twelfth Article of the Creed

130. What is the twelfth article of the Creed?

The twelfth article of the Creed is, 'life everlasting'.

131. What does 'life everlasting' mean?

'Life everlasting' means that the good shall live for ever in the glory and happiness of heaven.

132. What is the glory and happiness of heaven?

The glory and happiness of heaven is to see, love, and enjoy God for ever.

133. What does the Scripture say of the happiness of heaven?

The Scripture says of the happiness of heaven: 'No eye has seen and no ear has heard, things beyond the mind of man, all that God has prepared for those who love him.' *(1 Cor. 2:9)*

134. Shall not the wicked also live for ever?

The wicked also shall live and be punished for ever in the fire of hell.

❧ HOPE ❧

Hope and Grace

135. Will Faith alone save us?

Faith alone will not save us without good works; we must also have Hope and Charity.

136. What is Hope?

Hope is a supernatural gift of God, by which we firmly trust that God will give us eternal life and all means necessary to obtain it, if we do what he requires of us.

137. Why must we hope in God?

We must hope in God because he is infinitely good, infinitely powerful, and faithful to his promises.

138. Can we do any good work of ourselves towards our salvation?

We can do no good work of ourselves towards our salvation; we need the help of God's grace.

139. What is Grace?

Grace is a supernatural gift of God, freely bestowed upon us for our sanctification and salvation.

140. How must we obtain God's grace?

We must obtain God's grace chiefly by prayer and the holy Sacraments.

Prayer

141. What is prayer?

Prayer is the raising up of the mind and heart to God.

142. How do we raise up our mind and heart to God?

We raise up our mind and heart to God by thinking of God; by adoring, praising, and thanking him; and by begging of him all blessings for soul and body.

143. Do those pray well who, at their prayers, think neither of God nor of what they say?

Those who, at their prayers, think neither of God nor of what they say, do not pray well; but they offend God, if their distractions are wilful.

144. Which is the best of all prayers?

The best of all prayers is the 'Our Father', or the Lord's Prayer.

145. Who made the Lord's Prayer?

Jesus Christ himself made the Lord's Prayer.

146. Say the Lord's Prayer.

Our Father, who art in heaven, hallowed by thy name; thy kingdom come; thy will be done on earth as it is in heaven; give us this day our daily bread; and forgive us our trespasses, as we forgive those who trespass against us; and lead us not into temptation; but deliver us from evil. Amen.

147. In the Lord's Prayer who is called 'our Father'?

In the Lord's prayer God is called 'our Father'.

148. Why is God called 'our Father'?

God is called 'our Father' because he is the Father of all Christians, whom he has made his children by Holy Baptism.

149. Is God also the Father of all mankind?

God is also the Father of all mankind because he made them all, and loves and preserves them all.

150. Why do we say, 'our' Father, and not 'my' Father?

We say 'our' Father, and not 'my' Father, because, being all brethren, we are to pray not for ourselves only, but also for all others.

151. When we say, 'hallowed by thy name', what do we pray for?

When we say, 'hallowed by thy name', we pray that God may be known, loved, and served by all his creatures.

152. When we say, 'thy Kingdom come', what do we pray for?

When we say, 'thy kingdom come', we pray that God may come and reign in the hearts of all by his grace in this world, and bring us all hereafter to his heavenly kingdom.

153. When we say, 'thy will be done on earth as it is in heaven', what do we pray for?

When we say, 'thy will be done on earth as it is in heaven', we pray that God may enable us, by his grace, to do his will in all things, as the Blessed do in heaven.

154. When we say, 'give us this day our daily bread', what do we pray for?

When we say, 'give us this day our daily bread' we pray that God may give us daily all that is necessary for soul and body.

155. When we say 'forgive us our trespasses, as we forgive those who trespass against us', what do we pray for?

When we say, 'forgive us our trespasses, as we forgive those who trespass against us', we pray that God may forgive us our sins, as we forgive others the injuries they do to us.

156. When we say, 'lead us not into temptation', what do we pray for?

When we say, 'lead us not into temptation' we pray that God may give us grace not to yield to temptation.

157. When we say, 'deliver us from evil', what do we pray for?

When we say, 'deliver us from evil', we pray that God may free us from all evil, both of soul and body.

158. Should we ask the Angels and Saints to pray for us?

We should ask the Angels and Saints to pray for us, because they are our friends and brethren, and because their prayers have great power with God.

159. How can we show that the Angels and Saints know what passes on earth?

We can show that the Angels and Saints know what passes on earth from the words of Christ: 'There shall be joy before the Angels of God upon one sinner doing penance'. *(Luke 15:10)*

160. What is the chief prayer to the Blessed Virgin which the Church uses?

The chief prayer to the Blessed Virgin which the Church uses is the Hail Mary.

161. Say the Hail Mary.

Hail Mary, full of grace: the Lord is with thee; blessed art thou among women, and blessed is the fruit of thy womb, Jesus. Holy Mary, Mother of God, pray for us sinners, now, and at the hour of our death. Amen.

162. Who made the first part of the Hail Mary?

The Angel Gabriel and St Elizabeth, inspired by the Holy Spirit, made the first part of the Hail Mary.

163. Who made the second part of the Hail Mary?

The Church of God, guided by the Holy Spirit, made the second part of the Hail Mary.

164. Why should we frequently say the Hail Mary?

We should frequently say the Hail Mary to put us in mind of the Incarnation of the Son of God: and to honour our Blessed Lady, the Mother of God.

165. Have we another reason for often saying the Hail Mary?

We have another reason for often saying the Hail Mary - to ask our Blessed Lady to pray for us sinners at all times, but especially at the hour of our death.

166. Why does the Catholic Church show great devotion to the Blessed Virgin?

The Catholic Church shows great devotion to the Blessed Virgin because she is the Immaculate Mother of God.

167. How is the Blessed Virgin Mother of God?

The Blessed Virgin is Mother of God because Jesus Christ, her son, who was born of her as man, is not only man, but is also truly God.

168. Is the Blessed Virgin our Mother also?

The Blessed Virgin is our Mother also because, being the brethren of Jesus, we are the children of Mary.

168a. What do we mean by the Assumption of the Blessed Virgin?

By the Assumption of the Blessed Virgin we mean that by the power of God, Mary, at the completion of her life, was taken body and soul into everlasting glory to reign as Queen of heaven and earth.

168b. Is the Assumption of the Blessed Virgin an article of Faith?

The Assumption of the Blessed Virgin is an article of Faith because it has been solemnly defined by the infallible authority of the Church.

◆ CHARITY ◆

The Commandments of God

169. What is Charity?

Charity is a supernatural gift of God by which we love God above all things, and our neighbour as ourselves for God's sake.

170. Why must we love God?

We must love God because he is infinitely good in himself and infinitely good to us.

171. How do we show that we love God?

We show that we love God by keeping his commandments: for Christ says: 'If you love me, keep my commandments'. *(John 14:15: Matt. 19:16-19: Rom. 13:9-10)*

172. How many Commandments are there?

There are ten Commandments.

173. Say the ten Commandments.

1. I am Yahweh your God who brought you out of the land of Egypt, out of the house of slavery.

You shall have no gods except me. You shall not make yourself a carved image or any likeness of anything in heaven, or on the earth beneath or in the waters under the earth. You shall not bow down to them or serve them.

2. You shall not take the name of the Lord your God in vain.

3. Remember the Sabbath day, to keep it holy.

4. Honour your father and your mother.

5. You shall not kill.

6. You shall not commit adultery.

7. You shall not steal.

8. You shall not bear false witness against your neighbour.

9. You shall not covet your neighbour's wife.

10. You shall not covet your neighbour's goods.

174. Who gave the ten Commandments?

God gave the ten Commandments to Moses in the Old Law, and Christ confirmed them in the New.

The First Commandment

175. What is the first Commandment?

The first Commandment is, 'I am Yahweh your God who brought you out of the land of Egypt, out of the house of slavery. You shall have no gods except me. You shall not make yourself a carved image or any likeness of anything in heaven, or on the earth beneath or in the waters under the earth. You shall not bow down to them or serve them'.

176. What are we commanded to do by the first Commandment?

By the first Commandment we are commanded to worship the one, true, and living God, by Faith, Hope, Charity, and Religion.

177. What are the sins against Faith?

The sins against Faith are all false religions, wilful doubt, disbelief, or denial of any article of Faith, and also culpable ignorance of the doctrines of the Church.

178. How do we expose ourselves to the danger of losing our Faith?

We expose ourselves to the danger of losing our Faith by neglecting our spiritual duties, reading bad books, going to non-Catholic schools.

179. What are the sins against Hope?

The sins against Hope are despair and presumption.

180. What are the chief sins against Religion?

The chief sins against Religion are the worship of false gods or idols, and the giving to any creature whatsoever the honour which belongs to God alone.

181. Does the first Commandment forbid the making of images?

The first Commandment does not forbid the making of images, but the making of idols; that is, it forbids us to make images to be adored and honoured as gods.

182. Does the first Commandment forbid dealing with the devil and superstitious practices?

The first Commandment forbids all dealing with the devil and superstitious practices, such as consulting spiritualists and fortune-tellers, and trusting to charms, omens, dreams, and such-like fooleries.

183. Are all sins of sacrilege and simony also forbidden by the first Commandment?

All sins of sacrilege and simony are also forbidden by the first Commandment.

184. Is it forbidden to give divine honour or worship to the Angels and Saints?

It is forbidden to give divine honour or worship to the Angels and Saints, for this belongs to God alone.

185. What kind of honour or worship should we pay to the Angels and Saints?

We should pay to the Angels and Saints an inferior honour or worship, for this is due to them as the servants and special friends of God.

186. What honour should we give to relics, crucifixes, and holy pictures?

We should give relics, crucifixes, and holy pictures a relative honour, as they relate to Christ and his Saints, and are memorials of them.

187. Do we pray to relics or images?

We do not pray to relics or images, for they can neither see, nor hear, nor help us.

The Second Commandment

188. What is the second Commandment?

The second Commandment is, 'You shall not take the name of the Lord your God in vain'.

189. What are we commanded by the second Commandment?

By the second Commandment we are commanded to speak with reverence of God and all holy persons and things, and to keep our lawful oaths and vows.

190. What does the second Commandment forbid?

The second Commandment forbids all false, rash, unjust, and unnecessary oaths; as also blaspheming, cursing and profane words.

191. Is it ever lawful to swear or to take an oath?

It is lawful to swear, or to take an oath, only when God's honour, or our own, or our neighbour's good requires it.

The Third Commandment

192. What is the third Commandment?

The third Commandment is 'Remember the Sabbath day, to keep it holy.'

193. What are we commanded by the third Commandment?

By the third Commandment we are commanded to keep the Sunday holy.

194. How are we to keep the Sunday holy?

We are to keep the Sunday holy by hearing Mass and resting from servile works.

195. Why are we commanded to rest from servile works?

We are commanded to rest from servile works that we may have time and opportunity for prayer, going to the Sacraments, hearing instructions, and reading good books.

The Fourth Commandment

196. What is the fourth Commandment?

The fourth Commandment is, 'Honour your father and your mother.'

197. What are we commanded by the fourth Commandment?

By the fourth Commandment we are commanded to love, reverence, and obey our parents in all that is not sin.

198. Are we commanded to obey our parents only?

We are commanded to obey, not only our parents, but also our bishops and pastors, the civil authorities, and our lawful superiors.

199. Are we bound to assist our parents in their wants?

We are bound to assist our parents in their wants, both spiritual and temporal.

200. Are we bound in justice to contribute to the support of our pastors?

We are bound in justice to contribute to the support of our pastors; for St Paul says: 'The Lord directed that those who preach the Gospel should get their living from the Gospel'. *(1 Cor. 9:14)*

201. What is the duty of parents towards their children?

The duty of parents towards their children is to provide for them, to instruct and correct them, and to give them a good Catholic education.

202. What is the duty of masters, mistresses, and other superiors?

The duty of masters, mistresses, and other superiors is to take proper care of those under their charge, and to enable them to practise their religious duties.

203. What does the fourth Commandment forbid?

The fourth Commandment forbids all contempt, stubbornness, and disobedience to our parents and lawful superiors.

204. Is it sinful to belong to a Secret Society?

It is sinful to belong to any Secret Society that plots against the Church or State, or to any Society that by reason of its secrecy is condemned by the Church; for St Paul says: 'You must all obey the governing authorities. Since all government comes from God, the civil authorities were appointed by God, and so anyone who resists authority is rebelling against God's decision, and such an act is bound to be punished.' *(Rom. 13:1.2)*

The Fifth Commandment

205. What is the fifth Commandment?

The fifth Commandment is, 'You shall not kill'.

206. What does the fifth Commandment forbid?

The fifth Commandment forbids all wilful murder, fighting, quarrelling, and injurious words; and also scandal and bad example.

207. Does the fifth Commandment forbid anger?

The fifth Commandment forbids anger, and still more, hatred and revenge.

208. Why are scandal and bad example forbidden by the fifth Commandment?

Scandal and bad example are forbidden by the fifth Commandment, because they lead to the injury and spiritual death of our neighbour's soul.

The Sixth Commandment

209. What is the sixth Commandment?

The sixth Commandment is, 'You shall not commit adultery'.

210. What does the sixth Commandment forbid?

The sixth Commandment forbids all sins of impurity with another's wife or husband.

211. Does the sixth Commandment forbid whatever is contrary to holy purity?

The sixth Commandment forbids whatever is contrary to holy purity in looks, words, or actions.

212. Are immodest plays and dances forbidden by the sixth Commandment?

Immodest plays and dances are forbidden by the sixth Commandment, and it is sinful to look at them.

213. Does the sixth Commandment forbid immodest songs, books, and pictures?

The six Commandment forbids immodest songs, books, and pictures, because they are most dangerous to the soul, and lead to mortal sin.

The Seventh Commandment

214. What is the seventh Commandment?

The seventh Commandment is, 'You shall not steal'.

215. What does the seventh Commandment forbid?

The seventh Commandment forbids all unjust taking away, or keeping what belongs to another.

216. Is all manner of cheating in buying and selling forbidden by the seventh Commandment?

All manner of cheating in buying and selling is forbidden by the seventh Commandment, and also every other way of wronging our neighbour.

217. Are we bound to restore ill-gotten goods?

We are bound to restore ill-gotten goods if we are able, or else the sin will not be forgiven; we must also pay our debts.

218. Is it dishonest for workers to waste their employer's time or property?

It is dishonest for workers to waste their employer's time or property, because it is wasting what is not their own.

The Eighth Commandment

219. What is the eighth Commandment?

The eighth Commandment is, 'You shall not bear false witness against your neighbour'.

220. What does the eighth Commandment forbid?

The eighth Commandment forbids all false testimony, rash judgment, and lies.

221. Are calumny and detraction forbidden by the eighth Commandment?

Calumny and detraction are forbidden by the eighth Commandment, and also tale-bearing, and any words which injure our neighbour's character.

222. If you have injured your neighbour by speaking ill of him, what are you bound to do?

If I have injured my neighbour by speaking ill of him, I am bound to make him satisfaction by restoring his good name as far as I can.

The Ninth Commandment

223. What is the ninth Commandment?

The ninth Commandment is, 'You shall not covet your neighbour's wife'.

224. What does the ninth Commandment forbid?

The ninth Commandment forbids all wilful consent to impure thoughts and desires, and all wilful pleasure in the irregular motions of the flesh.

225. What sins commonly lead to the breaking of the sixth and ninth Commandments?

The sins that commonly lead to the breaking of the sixth and ninth Commandments are gluttony, drunkenness, and intemperance, and also idleness, bad company, and the neglect of prayer.

The Tenth Commandment

226. What is the tenth Commandment?

The tenth Commandment is, 'You shall not covet your neighbour's goods'.

227. What does the tenth Commandment forbid?

The tenth Commandment forbids all envious and covetous thoughts and unjust desires of our neighbour's goods and profits.

The Commandments of the Church

228. Are we bound to obey the Church?

We are bound to obey the Church, because Christ has said to the pastors of the Church: 'Anyone who listens to you, listens to me: anyone who rejects you rejects me'. *(Luke 10:16)*

229. What are the chief Commandments of the Church?

The chief Commandments of the Church are:

1. To keep the Sundays and Holy days of Obligation holy, by hearing Mass and resting from servile works.
2. To observe the appointed days of penance.
3. To go to confession at least once a year.
4. To receive the Blessed Sacrament at least once a year, and that at Easter or thereabouts.
5. To contribute to the support of our pastors.
6. Not to marry within certain degrees of kindred.

230. What is the first Commandment of the Church?

The first Commandment of the Church is, 'To keep the Sundays and Holy days of Obligation holy, by hearing Mass and resting from servile works'.

231. Which are the Holy days of Obligation observed in England and Wales?

The Holy days of Obligation observed in England and Wales are: Christmas Day, the Epiphany, the Ascension, Corpus Christi, SS Peter and Paul, the Assumption of our Lady, and All Saints.

232. Are Catholics bound to attend Mass on Sundays and Holy days of Obligation?

Catholics are under a serious obligation to attend Mass on Sundays and Holy days of Obligation unless prevented by other serious duties or by ill-health.

233. Are parents, masters, and mistresses bound to provide that those under their charge shall hear Mass on Sundays and Holy days of Obligation?

Parents, masters and mistresses are bound to provide that those under their charge shall hear Mass on Sundays and Holy days of Obligation.

234. What is the second Commandment of the Church?

The second Commandment of the Church is 'To observe the appointed days of penance'.

235. Which are the appointed days of penance?

The appointed days of penance are each Friday of the year and the Season of Lent.

236. What are days of Penance?

Days of Penance are days on which we are in a special manner to devote ourselves to prayer, works of charity and self-denial.

237. What are the Friday forms of Penance?

On Fridays other than Solemnities we are to abstain from meat or some other food, drink or amusement or undertake one of the other works of penance stipulated by the Bishops' Conference. (Abstinence is binding from the age of 14).

238. On Ash Wednesday and Good Friday what forms of penance are we to observe?

On Ash Wednesday and Good Friday we are to fast and observe the Friday forms of penance.

239. What is fasting?

Fasting is eating considerably less food. The Church commands us to fast and abstain that so we may mortify the flesh and satisfy God for our sins. (Fasting is binding between the age of 18 and 59).

240. How often should we go to Confession?

If we have been guilty of serious sin we should go to Confession as soon as possible, but never less than once a year.

241. How soon are children bound to go to confession?

Children are bound to go to confession as soon as they have come to the use of reason, and are capable of serious sin.

242. When are children generally supposed to come to the use of reason?

Children are generally supposed to come to the use of reason about the age of seven years.

243. What is the fourth Commandment of the Church?

The fourth Commandment of the Church is, 'To receive the Blessed Sacrament at least once a year, and that at Easter or thereabouts.

244. How soon are Christians bound to receive the Blessed Sacrament?

Christians are bound to receive the Blessed Sacrament as soon as they are capable of distinguishing the Body of Christ from ordinary bread, and are judged to be sufficiently instructed.

245. What is the fifth Commandment of the Church?

The fifth Commandment of the Church is, 'To contribute to the support of our pastors'.

246. Is it a duty to contribute to the support of religion?

It is a duty to contribute to the support of religion according to our means, so that God may be duly honoured and worshipped, and the kingdom of his Church extended.

247. What is the sixth Commandment of the Church?

The sixth Commandment of the Church is, 'Not to marry within certain degrees of kindred'.

248. Are there any times of the year in which it is forbidden to marry?

There are no times of the year in which it is forbidden to marry, but couples who marry during Advent or Lent should take into consideration the special liturgical nature of these times.

⚙ THE SACRAMENTS ⚙

Introduction

249. What is a Sacrament?

A Sacrament is an outward sign of inward grace, ordained by Jesus Christ, by which grace is given to our souls.

250. Do the Sacraments always give grace?

The Sacraments always give grace to those who receive them worthily.

251. Whence have the Sacraments the power of giving grace?

The Sacraments have the power of giving grace from the merits of Christ's Precious Blood which they apply to our souls.

252. Ought we to have a great desire to receive the Sacraments?

We ought to have a great desire to receive the Sacraments, because they are the chief means of our salvation.

253. Is a character given to the soul by any of the Sacraments?

A character is given to the soul by the Sacraments of Baptism, Confirmation, and Holy Order.

254. What is a character?

A character is a mark or seal on the soul which cannot be effaced, and therefore the Sacrament conferring it may not be repeated.

255. How many Sacraments are there?

There are seven Sacraments: Baptism, Confirmation, Holy Eucharist, Penance, the Anointing of the Sick, Holy Order, and Matrimony.

Baptism

256. What is Baptism?

Baptism is a Sacrament which cleanses us from original sin, makes us Christians, children of God, and members of the Church.

257. Does Baptism also forgive actual sins?

Baptism also forgives actual sins, with all punishment due to them, when it is received in proper dispositions by those who have been guilty of actual sin.

258. Who is the ordinary minister of Baptism?

The ordinary minister of Baptism is a priest; but any one may baptise in case of necessity, when a priest cannot be had.

259. How is Baptism given?

Baptism is given by pouring water on the head of the child, saying at the same time these words: 'I baptise you in the name of the Father, and of the Son, and of the Holy Spirit'.

260. What do we promise in Baptism?

We promise in Baptism to renounce the devil and all his works and pomps.

261. Is Baptism necessary for salvation?

Baptism is necessary for salvation because Christ has said: 'Unless a man is born again through water and the Spirit, he cannot enter the kingdom of God'. *(John 3:5)*

Confirmation

262. What is Confirmation?

Confirmation is a Sacrament by which we receive the Holy Spirit, in order to make us strong and perfect Christians and soldiers of Jesus Christ.

263. Who is the ordinary minister of Confirmation?

The ordinary minister of Confirmation is a Bishop.

264. How does the Bishop administer the Sacrament of Confirmation?

The Bishop administers the Sacrament of Confirmation by praying that the Holy Spirit may come down upon those who are to be confirmed; and by laying his hand on them, and making the sign of the cross with chrism on their foreheads, at the same time pronouncing certain words.

265. What are the words used in Confirmation?

The words used in Confirmation are these: 'N... be sealed with the Gift of the Holy Spirit'.

The Holy Eucharist

266. What is the Sacrament of the Holy Eucharist?

The Sacrament of the Holy Eucharist is the true Body and Blood of Jesus Christ, together with his Soul and Divinity, under the appearances of bread and wine.

267. How are the bread and wine changed into the Body and Blood of Christ?

The bread and wine are changed into the Body and Blood of Christ by the power of God, to whom nothing is impossible or difficult.

268. When are the bread and wine changed into the Body and Blood of Christ?

The bread and wine are changed into the Body and Blood of Christ when the words of consecration, ordained by Jesus Christ, are pronounced by the priest in Holy Mass.

269. Why has Christ given himself to us in the Holy Eucharist?

Christ has given himself to be the life and the food of our souls. 'Whoever eats me will draw life from me': 'Anyone who eats this bread will live for ever'. *(John 6:58.59)*

270. Is Christ received whole and entire under either kind alone?

Christ is received whole and entire under either kind alone.

271. In order to receive the Blessed Sacrament worthily what is required?

In order to receive the Blessed Sacrament worthily it is required that we be in a state of grace and keep the prescribed fast: water does not break this fast.

272. What is it to be in a state of grace?

To be in a state of grace is to be free from mortal sin, and pleasing to God.

273. Is it a great sin to receive Holy Communion in mortal sin?

It is a great sin to receive Holy Communion in mortal sin: 'because a person who eats and drinks without recognising the Body, is eating and drinking his own condemnation.' *(1 Cor. 11:29)*

274. Is the Blessed Eucharist a Sacrament only?

The Blessed Eucharist is not a Sacrament only; it is also a sacrifice.

275. What is a sacrifice?

A sacrifice is the offering of a victim by a priest to God alone, in testimony of his being the Sovereign Lord of all things.

276. What is the Sacrifice of the New Law?

The Sacrifice of the New Law is the Holy Mass.

277. What is the Holy Mass?

The Holy Mass is the Sacrifice of the Body and Blood of Jesus Christ, really present on the altar under the appearances of bread and wine, and offered to God for the living and the dead.

278. Is the Holy Mass one and the same Sacrifice with that of the Cross?

The Holy Mass is one and the same Sacrifice with that of the Cross, inasmuch as Christ, who offered himself, a bleeding victim, on the Cross to his heavenly Father, continues to offer himself in an unbloody manner on the altar, through the ministry of his priests.

279. For what ends is the Sacrifice of the Mass offered?

The Sacrifice of the Mass is offered for four ends: first, to give supreme honour and glory to God; secondly, to thank him for all our benefits; thirdly, to satisfy God for our sins and to obtain the grace of repentance; and fourthly, to obtain all other graces and blessings through Jesus Christ.

280. Is the Mass also a memorial of the Passion and Death of our Lord?

The Mass is also a memorial of the Passion and Death of our Lord, for Christ at his last supper said: 'Do this for a commemoration of me'. *(Luke 22:19)*

Penance

281. What is the Sacrament of Penance?

Penance is a Sacrament whereby the sins, whether mortal or venial, which we have committed after Baptism are forgiven.

282. Does the Sacrament of Penance increase the grace of God in the soul?

The Sacrament of Penance increases the grace of God in the soul, besides forgiving sin; we should, therefore, often go to confession.

283. When did our Lord institute the Sacrament of Penance?

Our Lord instituted the Sacrament of Penance when he breathed on his Apostles and gave them power to forgive sins, saying: 'Whose sins you shall forgive, they are forgiven'. *(John 20:23)*

284. How does the priest forgive sins?

The priest forgives sins by the power of God, when he pronounces the words of absolution.

285. What are the words of absolution?

The words of absolution are: 'I absolve you from your sins, in the name of the Father, and of the Son, and of the Holy Spirit'.

286. Are any conditions for forgiveness required on the part of the penitent?

Three conditions for forgiveness are required on the part of the penitent - Contrition, Confession, and Satisfaction.

287. What is Contrition?

Contrition is a heartfelt sorrow for our sins, because by them we have offended so good a God, together with a firm purpose of amendment.

288. What is a firm purpose of amendment?

A firm purpose of amendment is a resolution to avoid, by the grace of God, not only sin, but also the dangerous occasions of sin.

289. How may we obtain a hearty sorrow for our sins?

We may obtain a hearty sorrow for our sins by earnestly praying for it, and by making use of such considerations as may lead us to it.

290. What consideration concerning God will lead us to sorrow for our sins?

This consideration concerning God will lead us to sorrow for our sins; that by our sins we have offended God, who is infinitely good in himself and infinitely good to us.

291. What consideration concerning our Saviour will lead us to sorrow for our sins?

This consideration concerning our Saviour will lead us to sorrow for our sins; that our Saviour died for our sins, and that those who sin grievously 'have wilfully crucified the Son of God and openly mocked him.' *(Heb. 6:6)*

292. Is sorrow for our sins, because by them we have lost heaven and deserved hell, sufficient when we go to confession?

Sorrow for our sins, because by them we have lost heaven and deserve hell, is sufficient when we go to confession.

293. What is perfect contrition?

Perfect contrition is sorrow for sin arising purely from the love of God.

294. What special value has perfect contrition?

Perfect contrition has this special value; that by it our sins are forgiven immediately, even before we confess them; but nevertheless, if they are serious, we are strictly bound to confess them afterwards.

295. What is confession?

Confession is to accuse ourselves of our sins to a priest approved by the Bishop.

296. What if a person wilfully conceals a serious sin in confession?

If a personal wilfully conceals a serious sin in confession he is guilty of a great sacrilege, by telling a lie to the Holy Spirit in making a bad confession.

297. How many things have we to do in order to prepare for confession?

We have four things to do in order to prepare for confession: first, we must heartily pray for grace to make a good confession: secondly, we must carefully examine our conscience: thirdly, we must take time and care to make a good act of contrition: and fourthly, we must resolve by the help of God to renounce our sins, and to begin a new life for the future.

298. What is satisfaction?

Satisfaction is doing the penance given us by the priest.

299. Does the penance given by the priest always make full satisfaction for our sins?

The penance given by the priest does not always make full satisfaction for our sins. We should therefore add to it other good works and penances, and try to gain Indulgences.

300. What is an Indulgence?

An Indulgence is a remission, granted by the Church, of the temporal punishment which often remains due to sin after its guilt has been forgiven.

Anointing of the Sick

301. What is the Sacrament of the Anointing of the Sick?

This Sacrament is the anointing of the sick with holy oil, accompanied with prayer.

302. When is the Sacrament of Anointing of the Sick given?

The Sacrament of the Anointing of the Sick is given when we are in danger of death by sickness.

303. What are the effects of the Sacrament of the Anointing of the Sick?

The effects of the Sacrament of the Anointing of the Sick are to comfort and strengthen the soul, to remit sin, and even to restore health, when God sees it to be expedient.

304. What authority is there in Scripture for the Sacrament of the Anointing of the Sick?

The authority in Scripture for the Sacrament of the Anointing of the Sick is in the 5th chapter of St James (*James 5:14, 15*) where it is said: 'If one of you is ill he should send for the elders of the Church, and they must anoint him with oil in the name of the Lord and pray over him. The prayer of faith shall save the sick man; and the Lord will raise him up again; and if he has committed any sins, he will be forgiven.'

Holy Order

305. What is the Sacrament of Holy Order?

Holy Order is the Sacrament by which bishops, priests, and other ministers of the Church are ordained, and receive power and grace to perform their sacred duties.

Matrimony

306. What is the Sacrament of Matrimony?

Matrimony is the Sacrament which sanctifies the contract of a Christian marriage, and gives a special grace to those who receive it worthily.

307. What special grace does the Sacrament of Matrimony give to those who receive it worthily?

The Sacrament of Matrimony gives to those who receive it worthily a special grace, to enable them to bear the difficulties of their state, to love and be faithful to one another, and to bring up their children in the fear of God.

308. Is it a sacrilege to contract marriage in serious sin, or in disobedience to the law of the Church?

It is sacrilege to contract marriage in serious sin, or in disobedience to the laws of the Church, and, instead of a blessing, the guilty parties draw upon themselves the anger of God. (For the marriage of a Catholic to be valid there must be present (1) either the Bishop or the Parish Priest, or another Priest duly delegated, and (2) two witnesses).

309. What is a 'mixed marriage'?

A 'mixed marriage' is a marriage in which only one partner is a Catholic.

310. Does the Church encourage mixed marriages?

The Church does not encourage mixed marriages.

311. Does the Church sometimes permit mixed marriages?

The Church sometimes permits mixed marriages by granting a dispensation, and under special conditions.

311a. What does the Catholic partner of a mixed marriage promise?

The Catholic partner of a mixed marriage promises to do everything possible to preserve the faith and have all children of the marriage baptised and brought up in the Catholic Church.

312. Can any human power dissolve the bond of marriage?

No human power can dissolve the bond of marriage, because Christ has said: 'What God has joined together, let no man put asunder'. *(Matt. 19:6)*

‹ VIRTUES AND VICES ›

313. Which are the Theological Virtues?

The Theological Virtues are 'Faith, Hope, and Charity'. *(1 Cor. 13:13)*

314. Why are they called Theological Virtues?

They are called Theological Virtues because they relate immediately to God.

315. What are the chief mysteries of Faith which every Christian is bound to know?

The chief mysteries of Faith which every Christian is bound to know are the Unity and Trinity of God, who will render to every man according to his works and the Incarnation, Death and Resurrection of our Saviour.

316. Which are the Cardinal Virtues?

The Cardinal Virtues are 'Prudence, Justice, Fortitude, and Temperance'. *(Wisd. 8:7)*

317. Why are they called Cardinal Virtues?

They are called Cardinal Virtues because they are, as it were, the hinges on which all other moral virtues turn.

318. Which are the seven gifts of the Holy Spirit?

The seven gifts of the Holy Spirit are:
1. Wisdom   2. Understanding
3. Counsel   4. Fortitude
5. Knowledge 6. Pietys 7. The fear of the Lord. *(Is. 11:2.3)*

319. Which are the twelve fruits of the Holy Spirit?

The twelve fruits of the Holy Spirit are:

1. Charity   2. Joy
3. Peace   4. Patience
5. Benignity   6. Goodness
7. Longanimity 8. Mildness
9. Faith   10. Modesty
11. Continency 12. Chastity. *(Gal. 5:22)*

320. Which are the two great precepts of Charity?

The two great precepts of Charity are:

1. 'You must love the Lord your God with all your heart, with all your soul, with all your mind and with all your strength'.

2. You must love your neighbour as yourself'. *(Mark 12:30, 31)*

321. Which are the seven Corporal Works of Mercy?

The seven Corporal Works of Mercy are:

1. To feed the hungry.   2. To give drink to the thirsty.
3. To clothe the naked.   4. To harbour the harbourless.
5. To visit the sick.   6. To visit the imprisoned.
7. To bury the dead. *(Matt. 25; Tobias 12)*

322. Which are the Seven Spiritual Works of Mercy?

The seven Spiritual Works of Mercy are:

1. To convert the sinner.

2. To instruct the ignorant.

3. To counsel the doubtful.

4. To comfort the sorrowful.

5. To bear wrongs patiently.

6. To forgive injustice.

7. To pray for the living and the dead.

323. Which are the eight Beatitudes?

The eight Beatitudes are:

1. How happy are the poor in spirit, for theirs is the kingdom of heaven.

2. Happy the gentle; for they shall have the earth for their heritage.

3. Happy those who mourn: they shall be comforted.

4. Happy those who hunger and thirst for what is right: they shall be satisfied.

5. Happy the merciful, they shall have mercy shown them.

6. Happy the pure in heart, they shall see God.

7. Happy the peacemakers: they shall be called sons of God.

8. Happy those who are persecuted in the cause of right: theirs is the kingdom of heaven. *(Matt. 5:3-10)*

324. Which are the seven capital sins or vices and their contrary virtues?

The seven capital sins or vices and their contrary virtues are:

1. Pride.   2. Covetousness.

3. Lust.   4. Anger.

5. Gluttony.   6. Envy.

7. Sloth.

Their contrary virtues are:

1. Humility.   2. Liberality.
3. Chastity.   4. Meekness.
5. Temperance.   6. Brotherly Love.
7. Diligence.

325. Why are they called capital sins?

They are called capital sins because they are the sources from which all other sins take their rise.

326. Which are the six sins against the Holy Spirit?

The six sins against the Holy Spirit are:

1. Presumption.
2. Despair.
3. Resisting the known truth.
4. Envy of another's spiritual good.
5. Obstinacy in sin.
6. Final impenitence.

327. Which are the four sins crying to heaven for vengeance?

The four sins crying to heaven for vengeance are:

1. Wilful murder *(Gen. 4)*
2. The sin of Sodom *(Gen. 18)*
3. Oppression of the poor *(Exod. 2)*
4. Defrauding labourers of their wages *(James 5)*

328. When are we answerable for the sins of others?

We are answerable for the sins of others whenever we either cause or share in them, through our own fault.

329. In how many ways may we either cause or share the guilt of another's sin?

We may either cause or share the guilt of another's sin in nine ways:

1. By counsel.
2. By command.
3. By consent.
4. By provocation.
5. By praise or flattery.
6. By concealment.
7. By being a partner in the sin.
8. By silence.
9. By defending the ill done.

330. Which are the three eminent Good Works?

The three eminent Good Works are Prayer, Fasting, and Alms deeds.

331. Which are the Evangelical Counsels?

The Evangelical Counsels are voluntary Poverty, perpetual Chastity and entire Obedience.

332. Which are the four last things to be always remembered?

The four last things to be always remembered are: Death, Judgment, Hell, and Heaven.

THE CHRISTIAN'S RULE OF LIFE

—— ❧ AND DAILY EXERCISE ❧ ——

Rule of Life

333. What rule of life must we follow if we hope to be saved?

If we hope to be saved, we must follow the rule of life taught by Jesus Christ.

334. What are we bound to do by the rule of life taught by Jesus Christ?

By the rule of life taught by Jesus Christ we are bound always to hate sin and to love God.

335. How must we hate sin?

We must hate sin above all other evils, so as to be resolved never to commit a wilful sin, for the love or fear of anything whatsoever.

336. How must we love God?

We must love God above all things, and with our whole heart.

337. How must we learn to love God?

We must learn to love God by begging of God to teach us to love him: 'O my God, teach me to love you'.

338. What will the love of God lead us to do?

The love of God will lead us often to think how good God is; often to speak to him in our hearts; and always to seek to please him.

339. Does Jesus Christ also command us to love one another?

Jesus Christ also commands us to love one another - that is, all persons without exception - for his sake.

340. How are we to love one another?

We are to love one another by wishing well to one another, and praying for one another; and by never allowing ourselves any thought, word, or deed to the injury of anyone.

341. Are we also bound to love our enemies?

We are also bound to love our enemies; not only by forgiving them from our hearts, but also by wishing them well, and praying for them.

342. Has Jesus Christ given us another great rule?

Jesus Christ has given us another great rule in these words: 'If any man will come after me, let him deny himself, and take up his cross daily, and follow me'. *(Luke 9:23)*

343. How are we to deny ourselves?

We are to deny ourselves by giving up our own will, and by going against our own humours, inclinations, and passions.

344. Why are we bound to deny ourselves?

We are bound to deny ourselves because our natural inclinations are prone to evil from our very childhood; and, if not corrected by self-denial, they will certainly carry us to hell.

345. How are we to take up our cross daily?

We are to take up our cross daily by submitting daily with patience to the labours and sufferings of this short life, and by bearing them willingly for the love of God.

346. How are we to follow our Blessed Lord?

We are to follow our Blessed Lord by walking in his footsteps and imitating his virtues.

347. What are the principal virtues we are to learn from our Blessed Lord?

The principal virtues we are to learn from our Blessed Lord are meekness, humility, and obedience.

348. Which are the enemies we must fight against all the days of our life?

The enemies which we must fight against all the days of our life are the devil, the world, and the flesh.

349. What do you mean by the devil?

By the devil I mean Satan and all his wicked angels, who are ever seeking to draw us into sin, that we may be damned with them.

350. What do you mean by the world?

By the world I mean the false maxims of the world and the society of those who love the vanities, riches, and pleasures of this world better than God.

351. Why do you number the devil and the world amongst the enemies of the soul?

I number the devil and the world amongst the enemies of the soul because they are always seeking, by temptation and by word or example, to carry us along with them on the broad road that leads to damnation.

352. What do you mean by the flesh?

By the flesh I mean our own corrupt inclinations and passions, which are the most dangerous of all our enemies.

353. What must we do to hinder the enemies of our soul from drawing us into sin?

To hinder the enemies of our soul from drawing us into sin, we must watch, pray, and fight against all their suggestions and temptations.

354. In the warfare against the devil, the world, and the flesh, on whom must we depend?

In the warfare against the devil, the world, and the flesh we must depend not on ourselves, but on God only: 'There is nothing I cannot master with the help of the one who gives me strength.' *(Philippians 4:13)*

Daily Exercise

355. How should you begin the day?

I should begin the day by making the sign of the cross as soon as I awake in the morning, and by saying some short prayer, such as, 'O my God, I offer my heart and soul to you'.

356. How should you rise in the morning?

I should rise in the morning diligently, dress myself modestly, and then kneel down and say my morning prayers.

357. Should you also hear Mass if you have time and opportunity?

I should also hear Mass if I have time and opportunity, for to hear Mass is by far the best and most profitable of all devotions.

358. Is it useful to make daily meditation?

It is useful to make daily meditation, for such was the practice of all the Saints.

359. On what ought we to meditate?

We ought to meditate especially on the four last things, and the Life and Passion of our Blessed Lord.

360. Ought we frequently to read good books?

We ought frequently to read good books, such as the Holy Gospels, the Lives of the Saints, and other spiritual works, which nourish our faith and piety, and arm us against the false maxims of the world.

361. And what should you do as to your eating, drinking, sleeping, and amusements?

As to my eating, drinking, sleeping, and amusements, I should use all these things with moderation, and with a desire to please God.

362. Say the grace before meals.

'Bless us, O Lord, and these your gifts, which we are about to receive from your bounty, through Christ our Lord. Amen.'

363. Say the grace after meals.

'We give you thanks, almighty God, for all your benefits, who live and reign, world without end. ✠ May the souls of the faithful departed, through the mercy of God, rest in peace. Amen.'

364. How should you sanctify your ordinary actions and employments of the day?

I should sanctify my ordinary actions and employments of the day by often raising up my heart to God whilst I am about them, and saying some short prayer to him.

365. What should you do when you find yourself tempted to sin?

When I find myself tempted to sin I should make the sign of the cross on my heart, and call on God as earnestly as I can, saying, 'Lord, save me, or I perish'.

366. If you have fallen into sin, what should you do?

If I have fallen into sin I should cast myself in spirit at the feet of Christ, and humbly beg his pardon by a sincere act of contrition.

367. When God sends you any cross, or sickness, or pain, what should you say?

When God sends me any cross, or sickness, or pain, I should say, 'Lord, your will be done; I take this for my sins'.

368. What prayers would you do well to say often to yourself during the day?

I should do well to say often to myself during the day such prayers as:

Glory be to the Father, and to the Son, and to the Holy Spirit, as it was in the beginning, is now, and ever shall be, world without end. Amen.

In all things may the most holy, the most just, and the most lovable Will of God be done, praised, and exalted above all for ever.

O Sacrament most holy, O Sacrament divine, all praise and all thanksgiving be every moment thine.

Praised be Jesus Christ, praised for evermore.

My Jesus, mercy; Mary, help.

369. How should you finish the day?

I should finish the day by kneeling down and saying my night prayers.

370. After your night prayers what should you do?

After my night prayers I should observe due modesty in going to bed; occupy myself with the thoughts of death; and endeavour to compose myself to rest at the foot of the Cross, and give my last thoughts to my crucified Saviour.

— ❧ Some Common Prayers ❧ —

The Confiteor

I confess to almighty God that I have sinned through my own fault in my thoughts and in my words, in what I have done, and in what I have failed to do; and I ask blessed Mary, ever virgin, all the angels and saints, to pray for me to the Lord our God.

Act of Faith

My God, I believe in you and all that your Church teaches, because you have said it, and your word is true.

Act of Hope

My God, I hope in you, for grace and for glory, because of your promises, your mercy and your power.

Act of Charity

My God, because you are so good, I love you with all my heart, and for your sake, I love my neighbour as myself.

Act of Contrition

O my God, because you are so good, I am very sorry that I have sinned against you and by the help of your grace I will not sin again.

A Longer Act of Contrition

O my God, I am sorry and beg pardon for all my sins, and detest them above all things, because they deserve your dreadful punishments, because they have crucified my loving Saviour Jesus Christ, and, most of all, because they offend your infinite goodness; and I firmly resolve, by the help of your grace, never to offend you again, and carefully to avoid the occasions of sin.

The Holy Rosary

The Five Joyful Mysteries
1. Annunciation
2. Visitation
3. Nativity
4. Presentation
5. Finding in the Temple

The Five Luminous Mysteries
1. Baptism in the Jordan
2. Wedding at Cana
3. Proclaiming the Kingdom
4. Transfiguration
5. Institution of the Eucharist

The Five Sorrowful Mysteries
1. Agony in the Garden
2. Scourging at the Pillar
3. Crowning with Thorns
4. Carrying of the Cross
5. Crucifixion

The Five Glorious Mysteries
1. Resurrection
2. Ascension
3. Descent of the Holy Spirit

4. Assumption of Our Lady
5. Coronation of our Lady

The Divine Praises

Blessed be God.
Blessed be his holy Name.
Blessed be Jesus Christ, true God and true Man.
Blessed be the Name of Jesus.
Blessed be his most Sacred Heart.
Blessed be his most Precious Blood.
Blessed be Jesus in the most holy Sacrament of the Altar.
Blessed be the Holy Spirit, the Paraclete.
Blessed be the great Mother of God, Mary most holy.
Blessed be her holy and Immaculate Conception.
Blessed be her glorious Assumption.
Blessed be the name of Mary, Virgin and Mother.
Blessed be St Joseph, her spouse most chaste.
Blessed be God in his Angels and in his Saints.

The Angelus

V. The Angel of the Lord declared to Mary.
R. And she conceived of the Holy Spirit. Hail Mary, etc.
V. Behold the handmaid of the Lord:
R. Be it done to me, according to your word. Hail Mary, etc.
V. Pray for us, O holy Mother of God:
V. And the Word was made flesh
R. And dwelt among us

R. That we may be made worthy of the promises of Christ.

Let us pray.

Pour forth, we beseech you, O Lord, your grace into our hearts, that we, to whom the Incarnation of Christ, your Son, was made known by the message of an angel, may be brought by his passion and cross ✠ to the glory of his resurrection, through the same Christ our Lord.

R. Amen.

The Regina Cæli

O Queen of heaven, rejoice! Alleluia.

For he whom you did merit to bear, Alleluia.

Has risen as he said, Alleluia.

Pray for us to God. Alleluia.

V. Rejoice and be glad, O Virgin Mary, Alleluia.

R. For the Lord has risen indeed. Alleluia.

Let us pray.

O God, who gave joy to the world through the resurrection of your Son, our Lord Jesus Christ, grant that we may obtain, through his Virgin Mother, Mary, the joys of everlasting life. Through the same Christ our Lord.

R. Amen.

The Hail Holy Queen

Hail, holy Queen, mother of mercy; hail, our life, our sweetness and our hope! To you do we cry, poor banished children of Eve; to you do we send up our sighs, mourning and weeping in this vale of tears. Turn then, most gracious advocate, your eyes of mercy towards us; and after this our exile, show to us the blessed fruit of your womb, Jesus. O clement, O loving, O sweet Virgin Mary.

V. Pray for us, O holy Mother of God.

R. That we may be made worthy of the promises of Christ.

The Memorare

Remember, O most loving Virgin Mary, that it is a thing unheard of, that anyone ever had recourse to your protection, implored your help, or sought your intercession, and was left forsaken. Filled therefore with confidence in your goodness I fly to you, O Mother, Virgin of virgins. To you I come, before you I stand, a sorrowful sinner. Despise not my poor words, O Mother of the Word of God, but graciously hear and grant my prayer.

The Magnificat

My soul glorifies the Lord,
my spirit rejoices in God, my Saviour.
He looks on his servant in her lowliness;
henceforth all ages will call me blessed.

The Almighty works marvels for me,
Holy his name!
His mercy is from age to age,
on those who fear him.

He puts forth his arm in strength
and scatters the proud-hearted.
He casts the mighty from their thrones
and raises the lowly.

He fills the starving with good things,
sends the rich away empty.
He protects Israel, his servant,
remembering his mercy,
the mercy promised to our fathers,
to Abraham and his sons for ever.

The De Profundis

Out of the depths I cry to you, O Lord.
Lord, hear my voice!
O let your ears be attentive
to the voice of my pleading.

If you, O Lord, should mark our guilt,
Lord, who would survive?
But with you is found forgiveness:
for this we revere you.

My soul is waiting for the Lord,
I count on his word.
My soul is longing for the Lord
more than watchman for daybreak.
Let the watchman count on daybreak
and Israel on the Lord.

Because with the Lord there is mercy
and fullness of redemption.
Israel indeed he will redeem from all its iniquity.

V. Eternal rest grant to them, O Lord.
R. And let the perpetual light shine on them.
V. May they rest in peace.
R. Amen.
V. O Lord, hear my prayer.
R. And let my cry come to you.
Let us pray.
O God, the Creator and Redeemer of all the Faithful,
grant to the souls of your servants departed the remission
of all their sins, that through our pious supplication they
may obtain that pardon which they have always desired;
who lives and reigns for ever and ever. **R.** Amen.

A Morning Offering

O Jesus, through the most pure Heart of Mary, I offer you
the prayers, works and sufferings of this day for all the
intentions of your Divine Heart.

Aspiration

Jesus, Mary, and Joseph, I give you my heart and my soul.
Jesus, Mary, and Joseph, assist me in my last agony.
Jesus, Mary, and Joseph, may I die in peace, and in your
blessed company.